TH

50 ESSENTIAL QUESTIONS

AND ANSWERS

PAUL READ

FOR SOPHIE

WHOSE GRACE, POISE AND OBSTINATE NATURE

CONTINUES TO INSPIRE MY EVERY MOVE.

CONTENTS

ACKNOWLEDGMENTS

MY THANKS GO OUT ONCE MORE TO MY FRIEND IAN BETTS FOR HIS CONSTRUCTIVE SUGGESTIONS, ASSISTANCE AND ENCOURAGEMENT.

An Introduction

This small book came about for two reasons. Firstly, many students - both actual and prospective - tend to ask the same questions when starting a new course of Tai Chi. Over the 20 years during which I have been teaching, I have heard most of the concerns and preoccupations of newcomers to this art, so I decided to compile the 50 most common questions and attempted to answer them as clearly as possible. I hope that the answers will be a useful guide for anyone considering the study of this fascinating and profound art.

The second reason is due to the Internet. Since the phenomenal growth of digital content and the ease of information exchange from the 1990's onwards, there have been consistent claims from every corner of the globe as to what is - and what is not, Tai Chi. Consequently, it has become very difficult for anyone looking for a simple introduction to sift through the mountains of opinions, anecdotes and stories that proliferate each year on the Internet.

Discussion boards and social media sites are so overflowing with contradictory facts and information that anyone who approached the subject with an innocent curiosity would very quickly become confused and probably disillusioned by the number of arguments about authenticity of style, methods of practice and the importance of lineage.

To this end I have written this introduction. My hope is that it conveys some of the universal principles of Tai Chi and not just the particular approach of one school over another. I have tried my best to avoid all contested dates, figures and frequent points of contention. I have not always been successful, however, but I believe by focusing on that which unites the

different branches of Tai Chi, everyone can benefit from the simple guidelines and explanations presented here.

There are nine distinct chapters in the book, each attempting to look at one particular aspect of Tai Chi: from the basic questions about class structure and what the name itself means, to something on the history and the different styles and forms that are now taught. There are also chapters on the different applications of Tai chi: martial, health and energy use. The final section focuses on living Tai Chi: attitudes, ideas and 21st century applications.

Although the book has been written with a linear plan...section following section, I recognise that linear planning is not always the best idea, and that in these times of hypertext and the circularity of thought, it would be just as valuable to be able to jump from one idea to another. So feel free to do this, to dip into any section in order to take what is useful, and discard the rest.

If after reading the book, you crave more detail, and feel confident to go a step further in exploring some of the training concepts in greater depth, then drop by at **www.teapotmonk.com** to read about a contemporary perspective on this Noble Art, or get hold of  the companion book to this introduction: The Manual of Bean curd Boxing - Tai Chi and the Noble Art of Leaving Things Undone.

Feedback will always be helpful. You will find at the end of the book a list of contact points. Please leave comments, suggestions or enquiries at any of the on-line addresses you will find there.

As I often say to my students as they stumble from one posture into another: Stop for a moment, breathe easy and enjoy the journey.

PAUL READ

GRANADA, ANDALUSIA

LATE 2011.

QUESTION TIME

1. UNDERSTANDING THE BASICS

Q.1. Why learn Tai Chi?

A. Perhaps this is the question that begins our journey, but it is also the question to which we return again and again. Why learn, why practice and why invest time and energy into this most noble of arts? A single word answer is often "health". But health can be interpreted physically, mentally, spiritually, philosophically or even culturally. Throughout this book we shall be looking into all of these interpretations, but first let us try and see the larger picture.

When we begin to learn Tai Chi we embrace something unique in our lives. Tai Chi teaches us to slow down, to relax and to let things be. It teaches us that by emptying our minds we can find space to learn more about life than perhaps we thought. Often, we find this very difficult, as our culture does not always look too favourably on self-examination. However, in this instance, the little time we put aside for ourselves is genuine, qualitative time for ourselves and for our 'health'.

Time for replenishing the spirit, time for leaving behind the toil of daily activities, time to recharge, rebuild our strength and quieten the mind

Whilst the rest of the planet finds itself distracted by the communications age and consequently accelerates in order just to keep up, the Tai Chi practitioner slows down, steps back and watches as it all rushes by. S/he breathes deeply, and while s/he may be distracted by technology and the 10,000 things (see chapter on Tai Chi as a Philosophy), a Tai Chi practitioner's attention is also diverted pleasantly by the texture of sunlight, the path of the moon or the movement of wind moving over water.

All of these are reasons to learn Tai Chi, yet for many it begins, once more, with health. Physically, you are choosing to do something positive in life, something that will play a consistent, incremental and beneficial role in building your overall constitution, changing your posture, deepening your breath and improving your overall strength.

Finally, people all over the world are learning Tai Chi for it is good to learn something that will not disappear like a new gadget, a passing fad or like yet another fitness craze. Tai Chi has been around a long time and is getting more popular. In part this is because it is so open to all sexes, all ages and cultures. It is an art that you can practice today, and still be perfecting it when you are walking your last days on this planet. It is an art that is relatively cheap to learn, requires neither special equipment nor clothes, and can be carried with you everywhere you go! Imagine, if you will, an exercise and health regime in the 'cloud', which is always there, pushed down to you at any time, in any place.

Tai Chi is an art for life.

Q.2. What happens in a Tai Chi Class?

A. The best way to find out is to go and view a class. Find out where your nearest classes are and go and visit each one. Introduce yourself, say you are there to watch (or join in if invited) and just see what you think and how you feel.

What you will see is pretty standard, though there are variations of course, contingent upon the instructor and the style you choose. Most classes begin by running through a series of movements and exercises that introduce you to the varying aspects of Tai Chi. For example, a warm up usually involves movements that loosen the body, improve flexibility and begin to build an awareness of body-tension. These may be followed by visualisation exercises, specific breathing exercises or drills in certain techniques or parts of the form.

The instructor will not only be showing these exercises to the class, but also watching to see how students are picking up the movements, who perhaps is struggling, who is sprinting ahead and whether the aim of each exercise is being correctly transmitted. You may also see some walking exercises that will help reach a quiet state of mind before engaging with more detailed parts of the class.

Very likely, there will be a section where the Form is taught and practiced. Students will follow the teacher's movements, initially to emulate them, but in the long term to internalise the patterns and eventually to produce a version that will be unique to you. We are all different after all, and no matter how much we might want to copy another person, ultimately we must find and interpret our own way of movement. (For more on this theme, see Final chapter on Philosophy and Music).

There may be other sections that follow the Form, some of which may involve working with a partner: yielding, sticking, push hands, rooting are some of the most common.

Q.3. What does 'Yielding', 'Sticking' and 'Rooting' mean?

A. Yielding is simply the ability of the body to respond appropriately to incoming stimuli. Sensitivity is the key to be able to successfully yield.

Wang Chung-Yueh wrote:

"YOUR BODY SHOULD BE SO LIGHT AND NIMBLE THAT A FEATHER COULD NOT LAND ON IT WITHOUT BEING FELT, AND A FLY COULD NOT ALIGHT ON IT WITHOUT SETTING IT IN MOTION."

To be able to stay relaxed is the key, for in relaxation there are no tight muscles that block the messages that need to travel through you. Once upon a time, this was predominantly an aid to fighting. Now, the advantages of  learning to yield go beyond the combat arena, for yielding enables a practitioner to remain calm, centered, whilst still acutely aware of all that is happening and without being swept up in the reactions of others. It is often practiced by yielding to the force or push of another Tai Chi player, without losing your own sense of center and balance.

11

Sticking is taught in many exercises, including one called 'Push-hands'. Again, it teaches you to stay calm, relaxed and to interpret another person's state of being by maintaining contact. Through such contact, information about tension, breath, posture, anxiety and intention can be read.

Rooting is dependant on good posture and alignment, so that you learn better balance in movement and whilst remaining completely still. Rooting connects you to the ground. As the name implies it is about finding your strength not just in your own physical body, but also by interconnecting yourself with the immediate environment. This may be with the use of breathing techniques, visualisation work or some simple body dynamics.

Over time, these partner exercises, solo forms and postural and breathing routines will become familiar and slowly merge into one continuous exercise, not just in your class sessions, but in the rest of your life as well.

This is when Tai Chi gets really interesting.

Q.4. What does 'Tai Chi Chuan' mean?

A. Literally it means the "supreme ultimate fist". Now, this probably does not help you very much so we need to take a look at something other than the literal meaning. We need to explore some of the ways in which Tai Chi is has been defined, and how it continues to be defined by different people for different reasons.

The two words, "Tai" and "Chi" together, mean the unity of Yin and Yang, or in Taoist circles: the mother of the 10,000 things. See! I told you that literal meanings would get us nowhere! The "10,000 things" is really just a name used to represent everything from the lunar winds to the clippings of your toenails. It was a description used a lot in early Taoist texts, and although it's not necessary that you grasp all the philosophy of Taoism to learn about Tai Chi, it is useful to know some of the concepts, such as Ying and Yang and Wu Wei. We will look at some of these in more depth later. But for now it is important to remember that when these concepts are brought together, "Tai" and "Chi" they mean the ideas and not just the physical movements. Now, when you add the third name "chuan" to the first two, you get the complete name and the complete concept: T'ai Chi Chuan - The system of fighting based on the principles of the mother of all things.

There, clear now?

Q.5. What's the difference between Tai Chi, Tai Chi Chuan and T'ai Chi Ch'uan?

A. There are some people that answer: Who cares what the difference is, the important thing is what they are in themselves, not how they are written! This is an understandable point of view. But, to be fair, there are two points that do need to be raised here. The first is that you often see Tai Chi written with an apostrophe between the T' and the ai. Technically, this is the correct

spelling - otherwise the pronunciation changes from a T sound to that of a D sound. Can you imagine calling it Dai Chi?

However, despite this technical point, popular use seems to be ignoring the rule, ignoring the complaints of linguists and purists everywhere. Languages, one has to admit, adapt and change and in this case the simple use of Tai Chi - without apostrophe - to denote the practice is becoming something of a standard (outside the forums of activists and the training halls of the most traditional practitioners.)

Finally, the word 'Chuan' at the end of Tai Chi means fist and so the whole phrase 'Tai Chi Chuan' technically refers to the practice of Tai Chi as a martial art.

> "If you talk to a man in a language he understands, that goes to his head. If you talk to him in his language, that goes to his heart."
> — Nelson Mandela

Therefore, some teachers have singled out the shorter phrase Tai Chi to mean the non-martial practice of Tai Chi Chuan. But not all subscribe to this view, and this is where it can get even more confusing.

Given the complications listed so far, many people just use the description - Tai Chi - as it rolls off the tongue a lot better and is quicker to type than all those versions with tricky accents.

Now, we have just one more linguistic variation to look at. Then we can leave the subject behind us and move on.

Q.6. What about Tai Ji Quan and Tai Chi?

A. You may see Tai Chi Chuan written as Taijiquan or a variation thereof. Don't worry about this too much as it is still pronounced the same. It all depends on which transliteration of the original Chinese you are reading. Some systems favour the Tai Chi Chuan approach (Wade-Giles) whilst others favour the Taijiquan version (Pinyin). Followers of each argue about the merits of one over another, but perhaps they really ought to remind themselves that the only correct version is that which is written in Chinese. All other versions are simply translations.

In this book you will see the use of Tai Chi liberally scattered here and there without too much caution. This is because I do not really want to spend an inordinate amount of time arguing about the order of some letters in a word. (Something we have already spent far too much time on already) I'd rather focus on the concepts and ideas behind them. So, for the sake of simplicity and typing speed, Tai Chi is what you will see throughout the book - pronounced with a 'T' and meaning the practice of the whole thing (whatever that means).

There, that's the grammar section over with.

Q.7. Will I have to wear a Chinese Silk Uniform if I join a Class?

A. Although you do see quite a few practitioners wearing flowing silk uniforms, it is not obligatory. In fact some would say that is not advisory either. I'm a fan of flamenco music, but this doesn't mean I like to carry castanets in my back pocket, or keep a fan tucked up my sleeve. Unlike many Japanese arts that insist on you adopting uniforms and going though gradings to achieve different belts to mark your progress, Tai Chi is a Chinese art and therefore does not follow the uniform or belt systems historically adopted for arts practiced in other countries.

> "If it requires a uniform it's a worthless endeavor"
>
> George Carlin

Progress is neither linear nor colour based. It is circular, and skill level is marked by persistence and dedication, not by what holds up your trousers.

Q.8. Will I have to wear those Little Flat Black Shoes?

A. Many classes do indeed promote the idea of wearing Chinese slippers. This is for two reasons. Firstly, they like you to think you are doing something oriental by wearing clothes or shoes from another culture, and secondly, because they like to encourage you to feel the ground beneath your feet. Trainers and hiking boots may inhibit that sensation, so choice of footwear is important when you first start learning Tai Chi. Chinese slippers are also useful for developing a good sense of balance and rooting.

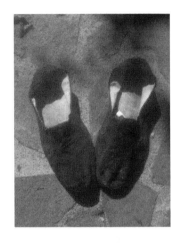

If you do buy a pair, they generally come with either rope soles or plastic soles. The difference is quite important: With rope soles you can slide about a lot more, the shoes are more flexible and less noisy when performing on your own in front of the whole class.

There is nothing worse than a beautifully executed form demonstrated to the accompaniment of a squeaky pair of plastic shoes. Plastic ones also tend to stick to certain floors making it difficult to do some postures, particularly the circle turns and kicks. So the choice is yours. Then again, if it's raining out, I know which I'd rather be walking back home in.

2. THE FASCINATING HISTORY

Q.9. Where did it all begin?

A. The History of Tai Chi Chuan is shrouded in myth and legend. It's almost impossible to get an objective overview of how the art has developed. Douglas Wile writes in his book 'Yang Family Secret Transmissions':

"ABANDON ALL HOPE YE WHO SEARCH FOR CERTAINTY...THERE IS NOT A SINGLE DETAIL THAT IS NOT THE SUBJECT OF BITTER SCHOLARLY DEBATE."

So if we put the disputed facts to one side, the legends and myths can perhaps tell us something else, something even more fundamental than the places and people that economics or politics have recorded for personal posterity. Facts are rarely objective. Dates and names may be, but the interpretations we place on them depend as much on who we are and why we are recording the information, as anything intrinsic to the data itself.

Perhaps it is the stories that will make a practitioner's feet "dance to the insights and inspirations of the words". (Douglas Wile again).

We suspect that a mythical figure existed at some point in the early mists of martial art history; a solitary figure who practiced the postures as separate moves, later unifying them into a unified form. We know that it was not until centuries later in the 'Chen Village' that the art we know truly developed, and it did not begin to spread out until Yang Lu Chan adapted it to a new era. We know that it was during the Chinese political and civil conflicts of the early 20th Century that the art was inspired to change again, eventually fleeing abroad to Taiwan and later the West where it would evolve again into something else for another people and another culture. More than this though is unclear. But that matters little when we look for inspiration rather than fact.

With that in mind, I present the -totally unsubstantiated - two-minute version of the History of Tai Chi Chuan. This version takes into account that we now live in a world suffering from attention deficiency and a world raised on a diet of social media updates and twitter length items and adjusts itself accordingly:

The Twitter History of Tai Chi in 5 Stages

STAGE 1: THE MONGOOSE

In the beginning, the world was composed of 10,000 things, mostly serpents and mongooses fighting each other in an unobserved manner. Later, a few human beings occupied the planet, mostly stiff and awkward types practicing single martial postures, not unlike those displayed by John Saxon in Enter the Dragon.

STAGE 2: THE PRITT STICK

Then onto the stage came Chang San Feng who was a keen observer of mongooses, and a dab hand at sticking together otherwise fragmented martial art postures. With his trusty orang-utan buddy, he fused the moves into a single simian form and changed forever the nature of the internal arts and the private life of the average mongoose.

STAGE 3: THE PEEKING

Several centuries later, in The Village of the Chens, the legacy of Chang San Feng was maintained to the point of incestuous absurdity, so that when a certain outsider named Yang Lu Chan 'the invincible', peeked into the Chen training halls, video-taped their secret routines and uploaded them onto YouTube via an open wifi signal, the secret was out at last. Astonished, the Chens dragged the Video-Peeker into their chamber where he reputedly 'whupped' the entire clan with one little finger and thereafter changed the direction of Tai Chi forever.

STAGE 4:

FROM INVINCIBILITY TO COMMERCIAL VIABILITY

The Video-Peeker's Grandson, Yang Chen Fu - a large and somewhat rotund figure - was burdened with the responsibility of continuing the lineage, so he peeked and learnt from the violent clashes of the Chinese Boxers and Foreign firearms so prevalent during the period. Observing so little invincibility, he contentiously shifted the balance away from Tai Chi Chuan - as the  Ultimate Martial Fist - to that of simply 'Tai Chi' the Ultimate exercise regime for all shapes and sizes. (Now Available on DVD)

STAGE 5: SHIFTING SANDS

After this, the world shifts gear and some bits of Tai Chi flee political change by going West. Some bits stay in Asia. Everything changes, however, because it is in the nature of things to do so. In fact, Tai Chi is built on such foundations and so effortlessly adapts to another time, language, culture and society. Sadly, it is then criticised for the next 50 years for it's very adaptability, as Chuck Norris-types all over the world fight to re-establish things the way they were, back before Mongooses were observed; a time when Tai Chi Chuan could be practiced in the style of 'The Village', thereby protecting us all from Weapons of Mass Information.

Q.10. Can you give me a more straightforward version?

A. Over the decades, practitioners such as Yang Shaohou, Yang Chengfu, Wu Chien-Ch'uan, and Sun Lutang have all contributed to the slow movement away from Tai Chi as a purely martial practice. At the time that Yang Lu Chan (the fence peeker) created the Yang style, he was a formidable boxer and took on anyone who would respond to his challenges. He became known as Yang Lu Chan the invincible, such were his martial skills. But it was not until much

later that one of his grandsons - Yang Chengfu - decided that an emphasis on health rather than the martial might better reflect the new and changing world of that time. So during the 1920's and 1930's he systematically re-wrote the Yang Style form, pushing much of the martial emphasis to the background.

Douglas Wile, in his excellent account of the Yang Secret Family Transmissions writes:

"THROUGH YANG'S OWN GENIUS...THE YANG STYLE OF TAI CHI CHUAN ESTABLISHED ITSELF AS THE DOMINANT INTERNAL SYSTEM IN CHINA. IT BECAME THE BASIS FOR THE NEW SIMPLIFIED TAI CHI CHUAN, ADOPTED IN CHINA IN 1956...AND IN ITS THIRTY-SEVEN POSTURE CONDENSATION BY CHENG MAN CHING, BECAME THE MAJOR OVERSEAS MANIFESTATION"

Of course when Tai Chi arrived in the USA in the 1960's it was embraced by a growing alternative social scene. This scene was to have a profound effect on how Tai Chi would develop over the decades that followed.

Q.11. How did Tai Chi arrive in the West?

A. It was due to a number of immigrants who started arriving in the West slowly, initially teaching only Chinese students, but later opening up their training hall doors to everyone. One of more famous of these immigrants was Cheng Man Ching.

It is said that Cheng studied with Yang Chenfu from around 1930 to about 1936. He is said to have ghostwritten some of Yang Chenfu's work that was later published as a book. It is generally accepted that Cheng was taught the most fundamental aspects of the Yang Style. Opponents of Cheng however claim he corrupted the art and taught only a diluted version to Westerners.

Despite this squabbling between stylists, we know that Cheng  Man Ching began to teach Tai Chi in China and began to work on his famous abbreviated version of the form there. This, many people mistakenly believe was developed by Cheng for a Western audience, because - so the rumour goes - Westerners lacked the attention span necessary to learn the long version of the form. This may be true, but it does not account for the fact that Cheng was already teaching his condensed version to Chinese students before he left for Taiwan in 1949. Like many other people, Cheng fled the new political regime in China, and so it was in Taiwan that he began to teach students in large numbers. Among them was a man called Robert Smith, who was working in Taiwan on a political assignment for the USA.

In 1964 Cheng moved to the USA, and with the help of Robert Smith, began to teach Tai Chi in New York. Cheng became one of the first instructors to offer training to North Americans and is remembered most controversially for the many changes he made to the Form. Among these was the concept of "swing and return", in which the momentum from one movement initiates the next. If you have ever seen Cheng Style you will understand how this concept applies. If you have not seen the man perform, then a quick search on YouTube will produce a few short videos for you to grasp the idea. Robert Smith meanwhile, went on to collaborate with Cheng, writing a number of important books on Tai Chi and producing several notorious books  about mythical fighting systems around the world under the pseudonym of J. F. Gilby.

It was not only Cheng Man Ching who brought Tai Chi to the West. Many other practitioners were beginning to teach in the USA, Canada and Europe at around the same time. But Cheng was certainly one of the more significant players in popularising the art in the 1960's and affording it the special perspective and following that it enjoys today.

One other US strand of development may be worth mentioning, and that is the Californian alternative social, political and arts movement prominent during the latter part of the 1960's. One example of this movement was the establishment of the Esalen Institute, which earned the support and participation of Alan Watts (the British philosopher) and the innovatory and charismatic Tai Chi teacher Al Huang Chungliang.

The efforts of people like Cheng Man Ching and the works of Alan Watts and Al Chuang still command a huge respect among many practitioners for their opening up of Chinese culture, arts and philosophy to the West. Their explanations and simple accounts of complex issues remain relevant, succinct and curiously timeless even 50 years later.

3. RECOGNISING THE DIVERSE STYLES

Q.12. What are the Main Styles of Tai Chi?

A. There are three main styles found across the world: Yang, Chen and Wu. Within each of these is a multitude of variations and nuances that are not of significant importance for the beginner student. In fact I'm not convinced that they are that important for the teachers either. As Mao said: "Let a Hundred flowers bloom". Were we to encourage this approach in Tai Chi, we would see an even greater diversity of styles that would perhaps address the needs of all those who tread the floors of training halls around the world.

But the world is not always as we would like it to be, and in the world of Tai Chi certain names or schools dominate the practice and the public image of the art. Some styles are seen as more traditional and pure, others as more recent with unproven modifications. Others still are considered outdated and increasingly antiquated.

Although you may think that selecting the right school is paramount, most styles share more in common than their practitioners would probably care to admit. Rather than fixate on names and categories, it would be better to remember that it is the teacher and the ambience of a class that will determine much of a student's progress, rather than simply a name or a possibly dubious historical time-line.

Every teacher will place a different emphasis on some aspects of a form over others, and in time these will ultimately distinguish their style from those of others. This is the nature of teaching and it is part of Tai Chi's rich legacy and development over the centuries. Some may deny this, others may embrace it. But rest assured you will always find in a class the fundamentals of the form: pushing-hands, rooting, breathing, Chi Gung exercises, sticking and yielding.

Q.13. How are the schools different from one another?

A. The Chen style, from which all others are said to have derived, still incorporates both fast and slow movements, as well as explosive and soft techniques. Other styles have leveled out these variations and tend to offer a more uniform pace in their forms and practice. The official modified Chinese form, and the original Yang Style have a much more regular flow and incorporate lower postures and angular stances.

Other styles such as Wudan and Wu still teach much of the martial side, while the popular Cheng Man Ching Form on the other hand tends to balance the martial with other softer aspects. This is notable in the Form's upright stances, softer moves and consistent flow with an emphasis on circularity. Fundamentally, the styles have come to reflect their teachers. Cheng Man Ching was called the master of the Five Excellencies as he was also a physician, painter, calligrapher and poet. It was perhaps his interest in other disciplines that contributed to his particular slant on the Form and practice of Tai Chi. I remember several teachers of mine that stressed the importance of knowing the acupuncture channels in the body. These people were trained acupuncturists or shaitsu practitioners and to them it made sense. Other teachers have trained in other martial arts and stress the applications of the postures.

As your teacher about their interests and you will often find why the Tai Chi school is the way it is.

Q.14. Which Style would be better to learn?

A. What sort of person are you? What are you looking for in a class? How best do you learn? Although we talk a lot about styles in Tai Chi, ultimately we do not, as individuals, fit neatly into pigeonholes.

Therefore in order to answer this question, you need to ask yourself: Are you someone who is practicing another martial art and wishes to complement it with something more internal?

Or are you practicing another martial art and would like to compliment it with a softer martial skill? Do you seek a method of meditation, or techniques for relaxation? Are you looking to build-up your immune system, or your muscles?

Whatever your answers to these questions, I always recommend that new students sit in on a class and just watch before deciding if it is right for them. Of course, all students can try out a class, but sometimes sitting to one side and observing gives an insight unattainable to the eager participant.

> "The important thing is not so much the style of martial art but the style of the instructor. Watch classes. Basic ones and advanced ones. See if it will match your preferences."
>
> Rob Colasanti

Through the act of watching you can see how the teacher interacts with the students, how well they follow his or her instructions, and you can absorb a little of the ambience of the class. If you are participating, this is difficult to achieve whilst intent on trying to copy the moves and postures of a new style.

After talking with the teacher, take some time to talk to the other students. Ask them how they feel about their progress and how they feel about the class. It has been said that the best example of a teacher's skill is the level of proficiency attained by the students, their attitude and openness to newcomers and their enthusiasm for practice. Try to see a little of this in each class you visit.

If you want to get an idea of how the styles vary stylistically, do a search on YouTube for the principal styles and you will see many examples of the different schools. This may also help when you finally find the name of a school that you hope to visit.

Q.15. Is it important to learn Tai Chi from a Chinese Practitioner?

A. Many people ask me about my teachers, and whether they were Chinese or British (like myself). The truth is, I have had teachers from many different countries and I can only respond by saying that nationality by itself does not convey good teaching skills.

Well, perhaps I should say that what is important is that you learn from someone who knows how to teach; someone who knows how to transmit ideas, concepts and actions and is a competent practitioner. It would be an error to select your teacher on grounds of race alone, although some people do think that it will give them a more authentic experience if they are taught by a Chinese practitioner. Authenticity, however, is not merely a matter of lineage, names or race. Authenticity is about how someone can relate, communicate and pass on experience, knowledge and skills.

In my personal experience, I have learnt form both Orientals and Occidentals. The only rule is to find someone with whom you can communicate. I learnt Tai Chi Sword from a Chinese teacher who used an interpreter in all his classes. This served to stifle somewhat the relationship between the teacher and the students, and made for very short answers to complex questions. Later I learnt from another teacher from Hong Kong who insisted on showing us a posture once or twice and who would then stand back and simply say "Do Again" every time we asked for clarification. It wasn't a helpful learning experience. Other teachers have had poor verbal skills but an energy and enthusiasm to impart knowledge that has more than compensated for the language limits. Each must be taken on their own merits.

Westerners do have a tradition of asking for details when learning new skills. They have a curiosity for information that is at times insatiable, and which is clearly part of our make-up. Perhaps this is not a bad thing, for in the long term this will benefit the spread and practice of the art.

Of course you cannot generalise from these examples regarding race, but the point remains an important one: Learn from someone with whom you can communicate. Communication may consist of non-verbal as well as verbal messages, but it has to be a valuable and satisfying experience for you.

4. LEARNING THE TAI CHI FORM

Q.16. What is the Form?

A. The Tai Chi Form is an important part of the practice of Tai Chi, but it is not the entire thing. It is a tool for practice but not an end to practice. Many confuse the attainment and completion of the form with the end of their practice, but Tai Chi is so much more that simply a list of postures strung together over a period of time.

This is not to play down the importance of the Form, it is in integral and fundamental part of Tai Chi. The Form consists of a series of postures that flow together, exercising body, mind and breath at the same time. It is said that before the Form existed, the postures were practiced separately as martial art moves (not unlike the many drilled techniques that are practiced today in most other martial arts). These separate postures were united by Chang San Feng - the mythological founder of the art - who fused them together in the flowing and uninterrupted sequence that we have come to associate so strongly with Tai Chi today.

Each posture of the Form has different applications regarding health and self-defence. Depending on the class in which you choose to learn, you may be shown one or both of these applications. In most classes, a new posture is learnt every week. The teacher will demonstrate the move from several angles, repeating it slowly with  verbal and visual instructions so that students can assimilate the subtle connecting points, and gradually build a familiarity with the posture. Each posture has a distinct order, so missing a class will mean that you may have to repeat a session or learn it in your own time. Either way, for many students some of the most difficult postures are simply those that they missed when the Form was taught.

Each style will emphasise slightly different versions of the moves, different numbers of repetitions or even different postures altogether. Despite this, it is still Tai Chi, and no-matter what your instructor says about the crucial importance of sequence and finer details, the truth is that the endless variations and subtle differences provide a fascinating tapestry and show just how much the art can adapt and evolve according to place and time. We should never get too obsessive about order and detail.

The endless repetitions performed when learning the Form may seem a bit pointless at times. But it is in their repetition that you can find the tranquility and grounding that Tai Chi offers and it is there where your Tai Chi studies really begin to deepen. The more you practice, the more you keep learning, the more you unravel and, like any language of the body or mind, the more you realise you have still to learn. Repetition and regular practice are crucial. It has been said that once you start Tai Chi, it's like a car's engine that ticks over if you practice often enough. If you do not practice regularly, then the engine stops, and you must work even harder next time to get it to start up again.

Q.17. What is the best way to learn the Form?

A. The best approach to learning the form is to empty the body of all tension, and the mind of all distraction. Through constant repetition the body learns much better than the mind, because our conscious mind tries too hard to grasp the facts and the details of the move. Our bodies, on the other hand, focus on the pattern and the feeling of flowing from one move to another. It is these factors that make a practitioner competent, not the ability to recall the angle of a foot or the inclination of an elbow strike. In order to promote this attitude, some teachers try to emphasise the fundamental rules rather than the strict geometrical positions. i.e. move with empty weight, keep the spine straight, when one part moves, all parts move etc. These basic rules can be found in what is known as the **Tai Chi Classics**, a set of principles (sometimes very abstract) that define the basic underlying rules of movement in Tai Chi.

The worst way of learning the form is to try and memorise it. Only using our head to understand, imitate and then reproduce co-coordinated body movements teaches us very little, other than how to copy. Although this might give the impression of learning, it is in fact no different than learning to draw by using tracing paper. A better approach is not to think, but just to flow with the moves; always keeping your eyes open and alert to what is happening around you. In this way it is not necessary to memorise anything. Just learn to read the moves, and trust your body to follow the patterns that will become increasingly evident the more you train.

Finally, one tip for learning the Form is to simply observe. Do not always try and do at the same time. Stop copying. Stand or sit to one side and watch the class go through a complete Form. Watch how the other students cope and how they interpret the moves and transitions. Do this regularly and you will gain an overall context for your learning that will feed directly back into your performance.

Q.18. How long does the Form take to learn?

A. How long do you want to keep learning? I once had a student who came to me from a Wing Chun class. He wanted to incorporate some of the lessons of Tai Chi into his fighting style and said that he wished to learn the short form within three months. We trained early in the mornings in an East London park, and over those three months he did learn the short form. His form was a reasonable copy of mine, but it said nothing about him. Nor was it particularly soft or circular. It became more linear, and punctuated by too many stops and starts. Some would say that he came to me with his cup overflowing, and never learnt to empty what he had. Consequently, it all got a bit mixed up and he ended up with a Wing Chun version of the short Form.

The problem with rushing a Form is that you only take what you see on the surface. What is underneath oozes out slowly, and only through the patient study of the subtleties and the recognition of the importance of transitions can you claim Tai Chi as your own. So why rush? What's the hurry?

The benefits are in the doing, not the acquirement of knowledge or movement. If it takes a lifetime to learn then you are indeed lucky, as the benefits will stay with you that long. If you speed-learn the Form, then you will only end up skipping the slow detail, and it is in the slow awakening of detail that the real benefits of Tai Chi are found.

Q.19. Are there different Forms?

A. There are indeed many varieties of Form, both in content and in length. Originally it was said that the Form had just 13 postures, and each was practiced as a separate movement. Over time the movements became unified, and this unified version spread to many different places where the many versions of the Form have since developed. Some Forms last as little as 8 minutes; others over 30. These numbers also depend, obviously, on how slow or fast your Form is practiced.

You may hear students talk about the long-form, the short-form, the old-form, the simplified-form, or the combined-form. You may hear or see performances of weapons forms and partner forms. You are also very likely to encounter the forms you will need to fill-in when you join a class. But don't let any of this 'form obsession' put you off. The forms are simply routines for you to practice in groups, or by yourself. The really convenient part of the Form is that it permits you to practice away from the class and thereby to slowly develop you own style. Do remember that the Forms are an important part of the Tai Chi class, but are not the whole thing. Practical partner work, including push hands and weapons training, can all contribute to taking your skill to a much higher level.

Q.20. Why bother with a Long Form when you can learn the Short Form?

A. Certainly the tendency these days is to focus more on the short Form. This may just be a reflection of our waning attention spans, or perhaps just a reflection of our multifarious commitments in this increasingly networked and interconnected world. Whatever the reason, the popularity of the shorter Forms have permitted people with less energy, and with less time to practice to learn Tai Chi. These shorter Forms remove much of the repetition present in the long versions. Cheng Man Ching said that you should practice his short form for between seven and twelve minutes to get the full benefits and I think this probably touches upon the real debate about Long - versus - Short Forms: it is really about concentration and focus, not the number of postures, that is important. You can practice the Long Form quickly and without focus, or the Short Form slowly and with concentration. Any instructor would rather see more of the latter than of the former.

This echoes some earlier statements on the quality of your practice, in that good Tai Chi teachers should be encouraging students to spend quality time during their practice; not simply counting the minutes or the postures. Skill and expertise comes about through a combination of dedication, persistence and patience. None of these qualities are confined to only one version of the Tai Chi Form. So, whether you study the Long or the Short, the Old or the New, the Combined or the Simple, do not worry. It is about what you bring into the Form that will ultimately account for the quality of your Tai Chi.

The long Form is well worth learning, but not at the expense of quality over duration. Always remember that Tai Chi is a tool that you adapt to where you are now. Then begin, and let the circumstances and energy roll you forward until the time is right to stop.

Q.21. Why should I practice in public?

A. There are two reasons why you should practice outside the class. Firstly, unless you learn how to employ the techniques to your daily life, Tai Chi will remain a simple past-time. In order for Tai Chi to become something more, you must practice at home, at work and even out on the street. There are many ways of doing this, and for those of you keen to see how to apply Tai Chi to your personal day then you will need to read the companion book: **The Manual of Bean Curd Boxing**. (See notes at end of book)

Practicing in parks, public spaces and many different locations helps to build confidence and familiarity with the moves. Practicing outside also marks the beginning of the process of internalising your Tai Chi. When you do The Form in public, you inevitably focus on how you are performing, how you are seen and what others may think of your performance. No one likes to do things badly or incorrectly in public as it does little to boost your self-confidence. One way of overcoming this sensation is to practice regularly. The first time is difficult, the second less so, and the third much easier. Over time, as you get used to people stopping, watching and moving on, your practice shifts inside and although you never close down the awareness of what is happening around you, there is an important change in where to place your focus and where to concentrate your energy.

Finally, learn to enjoy the sensation, because many people actually love watching the slow movements. It makes them feel relaxed too! Think of it as giving some of your newly acquired tranquillity to them.

Learn to pay attention to the animals around you. How do the birds respond? Do cats watch or hide? Do dogs bark or follow you around the Form? I once did a Form in the middle of a field in Southern England, and gradually all the cows at the other end started to drift toward me. By the time I had finished, I was completely encircled by a group of grass munching herbivores. It was wonderful.

The second reason to practice outside is to explore the different sensations that each location offers. Look for a place where the air you breathe will be fresh and invigorating, in contrast to that of an air-conditioned, or centrally heated room. Many students find that playing Tai Chi near trees or alongside running water increases the flow and presence of Ch'i (energy) in the body. Others have found that to practice just after it has stopped raining, during a mist or after a recent snowfall gives your Form a unique flavour. Each condition has its own qualities and can only be discovered if you practice outside of your bedroom

5. LEARNING TAI CHI AS A MARTIAL ART

Q.22. Is Tai Chi a Martial Art?

A. It is. However, this answer needs expanding upon because unlike almost all other martial arts that have maintained their fighting principles over time, certain styles and practices of Tai Chi have branched into other areas: health, meditative and philosophical. If you are a budding martial artist, you will need to find a school that advertises and promotes this combative element. Not all schools teach the martial elements, and some of those that do, only demonstrate simple Form applications and

techniques rather than sparring or competitive Tai Chi.
Remember, go and view as many classes as possible before
deciding on the one right for you.

What really distinguishes Tai Chi as a martial art is not so much
the range of techniques that you often find in other arts - specific
kicks, hand blows or combinations of moves - but rather the
emphasis on principles of relaxation, breathing techniques and
the development of internal 'Ch'i' energy. Collectively these
enable an approach to combat based
on the development of listening,
sticking, following, rooting and
yielding skills.

Most schools will teach these skills as
part of the Tai Chi curriculum, but
few apply them directly as a martial art. The advantage for many
students is that the principles are there to apply if they so wish.
And for those who would rather not learn the martial
applications, they can apply the principles to other challenges
they encounter in their daily routines.

Tai Chi - as an exclusively martial art - was more popular in the
19th and the beginning of the 20th centuries. But with the
increasing influence of Western ideology in China and the
recognised limits of martial arts as weapons of national defence,
the Internal art of Tai Chi began to adapt to a new and changing
political and social landscape.

Tai Chi became almost two distinct art forms. One maintained its martial basis, while the other opened itself up to the needs of other peoples and other cultures. Today, there are schools that teach Tai Chi as predominantly a martial art both inside and outside China. These schools insist that without the martial element, Tai Chi is simply another meditation technique and is out of balance with the all-important 'Tao.'

Non-martial artists reply by stating that the fighting elements counter the mind/body unity, which is achieved only through systematic and long-term relaxation, and that to devote so much time to learning personal self-defence in the 21st century is not only anachronistic but also feeding into a culture of acceptable violence. Like the yin/yang symbol, the issue is clearly neither just black nor white. What is evident is that, Tai Chi has evolved and continues to evolve by demonstrating its capacity to adapt to different needs. This is a healthy sign that it is an art that has a future.

Whatever school you choose, the martial skills can be useful in their non-competitive state. You can learn to read a situation well by observing the build-up of tension in another person. You can learn to step-aside before a situation gets out of control, or you can learn to present a non-threatening aspect to a potentially violent situation in order to defuse it by employing a quick body posture or smile. Rooting, yielding and sticking have their expressions in stance, posture, breath and attitude - any of which can be as useful a street survival technique as any other martial skill.

Q.23. Do I need to learn a Weapon too?

A. You do not need to learn anything you do not wish to learn. As we discussed in answering the last question, Tai Chi has a broad curriculum and can accommodate all types of students. Weapons are an interesting aspect of the art, offering Forms with straight sword, broadsword, staff and even fan. You may rightly ask: Are these useful skills for street defence? Are these useful skills for an urban dweller? The answer would have to be - no, not really, unless, that is, you habitually carry a sabre to the supermarket for slicing produce from the cheese counter, or plan to individually invade another country and 'fan' its population into subservience. They are, however, an interesting extension of your Tai Chi and the practice of wielding a weapon while maintaining your composure and balance can be a new challenge, as well as provide an opportunity to channel and focus your energy through an external object. It is also a lot of fun!

Q.24. But are Swords not expensive?

A. If you do like the idea of learning a sword version of the Form, but are concerned that enrolling in a weapons class may require a huge cash outlay for an original Samurai or Conan the Barbarian broad sword, then worry not.

There are a plethora of wooden swords, plastic swords or even broom handles available that will suffice in the early days of trial and error. Obviously a broom handle does not have the same weight, balance or feel as a sword, and neither does it slice cheese nor deter charging enemies, but it will afford you some time in which to decide whether a Tai Chi sword class is right for you without the expense of importing a hand-forged blade from Japan (or more likely from Toledo in Central Spain).

Q.25. What if I have no interest in the competing or the martial applications?

A. We are not living in feudal China, and neither are we normally called upon to defend our neighbourhoods with farming implements. Nor are we expected, in these times of computer aided warfare, to fight mano a mano for King and Country should war break out next week. As a mark of a modern and civilised society perhaps we ought to beat our swords into ploughshares, for today we are more likely to confront an enemy in the form of an unlabelled food additive on the shelf of a supermarket, than a knife-wielding gang on a communal staircase. We are more likely to be injured through fatigue, stress, contaminated vegetables or hormone-injected cattle than by way of the strike of a shuriken or the slash of a ninja sword. Therefore it makes a lot of sense to focus on the other aspects of this diverse and varied art. This is perhaps where the true strength of Tai Chi really lies: like the philosophy of Taoism, its principles and practice are different for each person, and so it flourishes in a thousand different ways.

We must also recognise that times change, and the needs for certain skills change with them. Typeface Setting is unlikely to be a skill that is in great demand for the foreseeable future. Neither do we see jobs advertisements for blacksmiths, milkmen and "rag and bone assistants" (A Londoners' reference there). This is because technology, social norms and social needs are changing the way we live and interact with one another. So it is understandable that not everyone sees the need to learn unarmed combat among all the other skills necessary in this new global village that we are constructing.

Yet there is still something about the martial arts that is not found in many other practices: these arts can teach us something of our vulnerability and not just our power. They can, if taught well, teach humility and compassion, as well as self-reliance and self-healing. They teach of the importance of spirit and attitude as well as of skill and accomplishment. The martial arts can present a balance of virtues rarely found in other learning disciplines.

However, you must make up your own mind. If you are not keen on the martial competitiveness, then simply pick a class that advertises itself as broadly health based. It shouldn't be too difficult, as these classes are very much in the majority in many Western countries. Whatever you choose, you will always learn the basics in any school and you can always change to another class if you would feel more comfortable elsewhere.

Q.26. So what are the other applications of Tai Chi, if not martial?

A. There are plenty of other uses for Tai Chi on the street other than simply defending oneself. Postural work, for example, can help a lot in defining how you move, the amount of energy you consume in doing so and how quickly you can recharge those batteries once your energy is expended. All this constitutes applied Tai Chi for it demands an organised and integrated approach to life using the principles of balance, movement and breath.

Then there are the mental aspects: how you respond to stress and anxiety? What happens to your breath and muscle tension when a stressful situation arises? How do you break out of the confirmation bias (repeated cycles of negative reinforced behaviour) in our everyday social exchanges? All these can be successfully countered by applying the basic principles of Tai Chi.

Finally, there is the philosophical application of how to approach the challenges of life, how to pursue your ultimate goals and aspirations, how to maintain and build your relationships, and how to integrate your spiritual needs in a world that appears to value only the material. All these can be explored with Tai Chi, and can prove to be hugely life changing, depending on your level of entry and desire to learn.

For more on this subject of 'Applied Tai Chi', see the Manual of Bean Curd Boxing

6. LEARNING TAI CHI AS A HEALTH ART

Q.27. Will Tai Chi help my Toothache go away?

A. Probably not. Neither will it help you develop bigger biceps, the stretching capabilities of Mr. Fantastic or a six-pack stomach. There are other exercise regimes that will better help you with such goals. As for the toothache, a less sweet diet and a visit to the hygienist may be a quicker solution.

Nevertheless, Tai Chi is often marketed as a panacea, which creates unrealistic expectations for new students. Stories abound of mythical instructors that healed themselves from serious disabilities or reversed the direction of incurable diseases. These accounts do little for the reputation and efforts of many good schools that cannot make such promises, for health is a very complex notion.

The concept of health relates to our notion of well-being, and well-being varies from person to person and from culture to culture. It is possible to live healthily, but not live well. Similarly it is very possible to live unhealthily, but enjoy a wellness elusive to many others. How is this so?

The answer has escaped health professionals for centuries; so don't expect to find the answer from me. However, we do know that the regular practice of a gentle exercise regime that teaches us good balance, good breathing habits, good postural mechanics, relaxation techniques and soft joint manoeuvres will help the body and mind to function in a more co-coordinated and health-promoting way. One of the few conclusions we can draw from the practice of Tai Chi is that it has a positive effect on your general constitution.

Q.28. This is all very vague; can you not say specifically how Tai Chi will improve my physical health?

A. In 2003 a study was carried out at the University of California that found a white cell count increase in practitioners of Tai Chi. This could account for the claims that Tai Chi players are better able to fight off certain infectious diseases.

There have also been studies related to the ability of third age practitioners to improve their balance and therefore reduce the risk of falls. Given the emphasis in Tai Chi on coordination, careful stepping, structural and postural work though, this is not too surprising.

Other Studies have also shown that a Tai Chi workout burns the same calories as surfing, horse riding and even light stationary bicycle training. This, I do find a little surprising but it would all depend on the nature of the exercises and drills performed in class. In theory it would be possible, though in practice such sustained aerobic activity would be unusual in a normal class.

Whatever the results of these tests - and most are vague and hotly debated - most practitioners will soon discover the benefits of their art. Speak to the many people who have been practising over the years and you will find a pretty similar story: Circulatory improvement, an increase in strength and lung capacity and the flexibility of ligaments and tendons, enhanced immunology, greater energy, awareness and powers of concentration, a sharper and more focused attitude etc.

In terms of simple physical strength, our energy derives from sources other than just our muscles. Tai Chi works on developing the tensile strength of the ligaments and tendons. They do more of the work in the class and take much of the body weight in movement. This is what accounts for the sense of gliding and smoothness in the form, which is what makes the postures blend into one another. The subtle shifts in where we place our weight and how we use our joints contribute to maintaining our overall strength, despite the inevitable atrophy of muscle tissue as we age.

Q.29. What about my 96 year-old Aunt? She says she want to learn too, can she come to the Class?

A. Age need not be a restriction to the practice of Tai Chi. In fact the benefits for third age practitioners are well known. Arthritis sufferers have reported relief and improvement from the subtle and gentle articulations of the joints, and asthma sufferers have reported easier breathing due to the specific abdominal breathing techniques and learning to co-ordinate their movements. There have been cases showing that third age Tai Chi players enjoy better mental health, feel better and remain more positive. All such claims are inevitably difficult to prove objectively, despite the increasing number of scientific studies. Yet, if you were to ask a teacher who has been giving classes for more than a few years, you would find similar answers: that Tai Chi is a wonderful activity for the elderly and, like learning a language, it is constantly stimulating, challenging and empowering.

Of course, when recommending a style of Tai Chi to your aunt, you may have to ensure that you do not enroll her in the contact tournament class or the weapons form course. She may find the relaxation and Chi Gung (see next section) exercises more appropriate. Once again, It is always best to view a class before joining and to talk about your - or your Aunt's - specific needs with the teacher first. Better still, talk to some of the students too, for they are a living example of what the teacher can teach.

Q.30. What about my two-year-old Niece, is there an optimal Age to start learning Tai Chi?

A. Children are not prohibited from studying Tai Chi and they often find many partner exercises enjoyable and fascinating. But in my experience of giving demonstrations in schools, you need to think about a specific approach for kids...for their needs are different from those of adults. Many adults come to Tai Chi with health issues, or to search for a tool to help them de-stress in their increasingly pressured lives. Children come because their parents push them into a class. The reasons are very different and therefore a class has to be designed around the needs of those attending. This is a general rule of Tai Chi: don't look for a style or school, look for a class that addresses your needs and start there.

Q.31. I have heard it said that Tai Chi is a form of "Moving Meditation". What does this mean?

A. Tai Chi has often been described as 'Meditation in Movement' because the focus on pace, slow movements, co-ordination of breath and posture and the gentleness and circularity of the movements can create an almost meditative state in which other concerns, worries or anxieties are pushed firmly to the background. This process begins the moment you step into a class, for uniquely in the practice of Tai Chi, the benefits of tranquillity arise from both the long-term aims and the moment-by-moment practice. It is both a means and an end.

"Cutting-off" for a short while and concentrating on physical and respiratory co-ordination also means that when the class is over and the student returns to the world of 'dust and distraction', s/he does so with a greater clarity and calmness with which to tackle the stresses and strains of contemporary living. So,  the benefits are not confined solely to the classroom, especially if practice is continued at home between classes.

Some classes of Tai Chi engage in specific meditation exercises. Some use guided visualisation exercises. Some just focus on Chi Gung work. Others transmit a sense of continuous tranquillity and meditation throughout the class. If this element is fundamental for you, then go and watch some teachers practicing, for will know when you have found a good one. Watch a good performance of The Form, and you too will feel calmer and re-energised. Imagine how you will feel when you doing the form!

Q.32. Why do my Knees Ache after practice?

A. Many people report that their knees begin to ache during the first few months of practising Tai Chi. This is predominantly because the movements of Tai Chi must be performed with sunken postures, with weight transferred to the lower half of the body, and with the knees flexed throughout the class. Consequently, teachers will tell you that this is to be expected and that the aches will pass in time. There is some truth in this reply, but it does not reflect the whole issue and ignores one aspect of Tai Chi practice that is often taught poorly: Structural Fitness and body mechanics.

It is expected that keeping your joints open, bending the knees and carrying the body weight on your leg muscles during the whole class will cause this initial ache in the tendons and ligaments. But over time, as these fibres around the joint strengthen, this ache normally disappears. However, if the pain in the knee is coming from the joint rather than the tendons and ligaments, or the muscles of the thigh or calf, then there is another issue to be resolved. Try to run through this checklist to see from where the problem is arising:

1. Try to keep you knee flexed during the class, but keep the knee over the foot. Don't allow it to go beyond the toes as you sink from one posture into another.

2. Avoid twisting your knee in the weight-bearing leg, particularly knee-twists that cave the joint inwards.

3. Avoid changing the position of the foot whilst carrying the weight of the body in that leg.

4. If your knees hurt then stop doing the movement that you believe is causing the pain. Investigate. Ask. Enquire. Adapt if necessary.

5. If you suffer with a knee weakness, think about choosing a style with more upright postures. Cheng-Man Ching Style might be a better choice for your needs.

7. ENERGY SOURCES IN TAI CHI

Q.33. What is Ch'i Energy?

A. This is a difficult question. Literally it means the 'vapour that rises from cooked grain'. But, as usual, literal definitions do little to help us grasp the concept.

What Some People say it is:

"IT IS A CHINESE WORD FOR A CHINESE CONCEPT IN WHICH MAN IS NOT A SEPARATE, DISTINCT AND UNIQUELY POWERFUL ASPECT

OF THE COSMOS, BUT IS IN REALITY AN INTEGRAL PART OF THE TOTAL."

...Michael Page

"IT IS NOT NERVOUS TENSION AND NOT PHONEY MENTAL WISHING. IT IS SUBTLE AND POWERFUL, AND CIRCULATES CONTINUOUSLY IN ONE MENTAL/PHYSICAL SELF. ACUPUNCTURE MERIDIANS SHOW THE PATH OF THIS CH'I ENERGY".

...Al Chung-liang Huang

Ch'i in Different Disciplines

The concept exists in Acupuncture where Ch'i is seen as a vital force that must be kept in balance, and allowed an unimpeded circulation in the body for good health. In Tai Chi it is the driving force of our strength, the power behind our gentleness and the presence behind our stillness. It is often felt as a tingling in the body, a warmth or even something as powerful as a wave or pulse of energy moving through the body. In Taoism it is the fundamental principal of change in the universe.

What do I say it is? If we see Tai Chi as a system of communication…using your body, breath and mind to understand, interpret and build a dialogue with everything around you and everything that you do, then Ch'i is the vocabulary of that language.

I understand that all this may appear too vague, but how do you explain a Chinese concept in English? How do I explain what 'gazpacho' tastes like to visitors in my country without using Spanish terms? Because without sitting in the shade of an old eucalyptus tree in mid-summer - when nothing is stirring other than a dog shuffling between shade and sun, and the ice is melting too rapidly on the inside of your gazpacho glass - such descriptions are almost impossible.

Q.34. Where is this Ch'i?

A. Some say it's in the cosmos, others say it's in your 'Tan Tien'…the home of Ch'i that resides just below your belly button, and a few centimeters in.

Others talk about it in your breath on a cold morning, in the sinews of your body or in your blood. Others refer to it in the clouds and the atmosphere. Some say that it all depends on what sort of Ch'i you are referring to, but this only complicates matters even more. To keep it simple, let us just say that Ch'i is energy and it is not only all around us, but within us too.

Q.35. Is it the same as the energy channels my Acupuncturist talks about?

A. Yes. This is not a new concept or one that is confined to Tai Chi only. Acupuncture is over 2,000 years old and, like shiatsu, focuses on this energy, manipulating it and harnessing it in order to heal the body. The channels though which the Ch'i moves are called meridians. If you imagine your body as being connected by an underground railway system, and the acupuncture points are stations along the route, you will be able to appreciate the need to keep the tracks clear of obstacles, and the stations open for the whole system to work well. There are 367 points in the body and all must be kept in an optimum state.

Q.36: What is Chi Gung?

A. Chi Gung (also written as qigong) is a popular form of health practice in its own right, but still taught as a part of the Tai Chi curriculum in many schools. Postures and movements are simple and repetitive, allowing the practitioner to focus on issues other than memory and movement. For this reason many students of Tai Chi learn these patterns much quicker than the postures of the Form.

Unlike jogging, cycling or ping-pong, Chi Gung demands your complete attention as you practice the moves. This is not to say that you can become an expert ping-pong player without giving attention to what you do, rather that in Chi Gung you have to develop an awareness of what is going on both outside and inside your body, slowly developing this awareness to be able to follow the movements of energy, and ultimately, to direct the energy itself. Breathing must be deep and from the abdomen. Movements must be slow and gentle with an awareness of body weight and body tension. Without this focus and concentration the exercise defaults to a simple form of calisthenics.

8. TAI CHI AS A LIVING PHILOSOPHY

Q.37. What has Philosophy to do with Tai Chi?

A. So far we have looked at the martial applications and the health aspects of Tai Chi, but here we are going to focus on the philosophical approaches to Tai Chi as a tool for efficient daily living

In a sense, Tai Ch is as much an applied philosophy, as an applied martial or health art. It attempts to unite the different elements of physical action, mental attitude and spiritual awareness in one discipline.

Because of these distinct parts, some practitioners have chosen to focus on just one element or another. Hence we have the incessant debates between schools as to what is and what is not 'complete' Tai Chi.

But Tai Chi is more than a definition. It is a balance of all we have looked at so far, and behind this concept of balance is the philosophy of Taoism and the Tao Te Ching.

Lao Tzu, the legendary author of the Tao Te Ching, tried to shift the focus of life away from systems of belief and instead towards the truth of experience. Accept what is, yield to it and learn from the moment, was his advice. Do not fight the world when it does not meet with your expectations. Yield, and in so doing learn the lessons of the strength of suppleness, the advantages of softness and the unstoppable force of water.

Q.38. Should I 'Be like Water my Friend'?

A. Not in the wet sense, but yes...in the sense of fluidity and adaptability.

One of the major concepts that Tai Chi uses is that of the soft overcoming the hard, and the clearest example of this in nature, is that of water.

As Lao Tzu wrote in the Tao Te Ching:

"WATER IS FLUID, SOFT, AND YIELDING. BUT WATER WILL WEAR AWAY ROCK, WHICH IS RIGID AND CANNOT YIELD. AS A RULE, WHATEVER IS FLUID, SOFT, AND YIELDING WILL OVERCOME WHATEVER IS RIGID AND HARD."

Softness is the essence here, and slowly the paradox of softness and strength becomes obvious in the practice of Tai Chi. The state of awareness while practicing is considered soft, but this does not mean it is floppy or weak.

The Chinese name for the concept is 'sung', and this means loose but alert, relaxed but poised.

However, in Taoist terms it is the fundamental quality of yielding than enables one to succeed. Giving way is not seen as a weakness; rather it is an act of humility and generosity from a position of strength, composure and an awareness of Wu Wei.

Q.39. Wu Who?

A. Wu Wei or non-action is a Taoist concept that is often badly translated as 'not doing'. But Wu Wei does not speak to us of an empty passiveness towards life, nor of seeking a refuge from the world. Think of the concept of 'sung'. Think of the Tai Chi hand: that gentle, flowing, soft and yielding part of the body that can stroke, caress, tickle, strike, gouge and punch. All depends on acting appropriately and with patience and timing.

To follow the path of the Tao is what is important, not by forcing a result but by yielding and flowing until the moment is right. When the moment is right it will be time to act with all the power and energy that is available to a Tai Chi player who knows how to respond from a point of centered-ness, stillness and calm.

Wu Wei is visible all around us, if we just know where to look. It can even be found in social movements such as Voluntary Simplicity and the Less is More movement. Politically, when the timing is right you can see expressions of it in the calls for change in the middle-east, or in the 15M demonstrations in Spain as people spontaneously, yet in an interconnected fashion, take to the streets to demand change. Seen through the eyes of a Tai Chi practitioner, it all could be said to have its roots in this ancient Chinese philosophy.

Q.40. Why would I want to do with Less? We live in a Consumerist Society. Give me More!

A. If you have ever felt that the information age was just a little overloaded, then buckle up for the ride of your life! The exponential changes that accompany the advances in technology will mean that we will witness the equivalent of 20,000 years of progress over the next 100.

If you haven't got the means or techniques to cope with such a pace now, then start learning about the benefits of cutting back and slowing down.

Slowing Down

This age of unlimited information has turned us into digital junkies, addicted to the zeros and ones that keep us updated, notified and connected, as if this digital fix will answer our most profound questions, such as: Why can I not just be still?

Unable to answer, we split our attention into ever-smaller pieces so that we are in a state of perpetual distraction. Smaller and smaller items of distraction enable us to maintain a hundred conversations at the same time: but they are all limited to 140 characters each.

If, however, we learn to slow down - or at least reduce our levels of consumption - we give ourselves space to see not just where we are, but where we are going. And who knows, maybe we'll even see something of the benefits of being still.

Q.41. Where does the Yin Yang Symbol fit into all of this?

A. At the beginning of this book, we looked at the meaning of the phrase Tai Chi and saw that one of its definitions was that of the joint movement of the Yin and Yang elements that make up this iconic black and white circle. The concepts go back over 3,000 years and explore the idea of opposites being complimentary and not antagonistic.

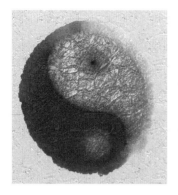

If we look at the world in this way, recognising the role that different sides play in the continuation of the whole, we see that there is much more room for participation, than if we continuously interpret the world as two sides, two energies or two enemies.

Originally, the dark element was representative of the shady side of a mountain, and the white element the sunny side. These concepts grew to take on the Chinese philosophy of dualism wherein all things were composed of two parts, each intrinsically entwined with the other. Some people saw the two elements in locked combat, others in an embrace of love.

Like Tai Chi in the 1960's, the Yin yang symbol became adopted as a symbol of opposition to rampant consumerism, competition and warfare. Its simple symbol of two interlocking fish has become one of the great icons of the last century and continues to have as much significance and relevance today as at any point in its history

Q.42. What is the Book of Changes about?

A. The Book of changes, or I Ching, is a collective text begun some 5,000 years ago and employed by businesses, emperors and academics to plot their strategies through life. Called by some an almanac, an oracle or simply a book of divination, it is composed of 64 hexagrams with lines that are interpreted by tossing coins or yarrow sticks into the air and observing the pattern they create upon their fall. The patterns recorded comprise either a dash or a zero, mirroring once more the cycle of life and the binary code that constitutes so much of our present day existence.

Does it work? Does it make sense? What purpose is there to consulting an oracle? These questions are difficult to answer with words. You can but try it and see if it works for you. The act of throwing coins or yarrow sticks merely connects you with a process that is underway and all around you (The Tao). Through more manipulative or controllable actions, you would find the results somewhat less useful. If you are keen to give it a try, be aware that some of the I Ching versions have more of a Confucian and less of a Taoist interpretation.

Q.43. What about the other classic book, The Tao Te Ching?

A. The Tao Te Ching is without doubt the cornerstone of Taoism, written, it is said by the old man himself, Lao Tsu. Legend has him born during the 6th century B.C. at 81 years old and with ten toes on each foot. He became keeper of the imperial archives at Loyang in the province of Honan, and in a fit of despair at the future of mankind, fled the decay and corruption of city life to become an immortal. He was reportedly stopped by a gatekeeper and asked to record down his thoughts for later generations.

Well, that's the story anyway.

The Tao Te Ching contains 81 poetic chapters on the essence of being. Undoubtedly, you will have heard many of these words quoted and re-quoted ad infinitum. But no matter how often they are written, there remains a contemporary freshness and relevance to their simple wisdom:

YIELD AND OVERCOME;

BEND AND BE STRAIGHT;

EMPTY AND BE FULL;

WEAR OUT AND BE NEW;

HAVE LITTLE AND GAIN;

HAVE MUCH AND BE CONFUSED.

And then there is the unforgettable...

HE WHO STANDS ON TIPTOE IS NOT STEADY.

KNOWING OTHERS IS WISDOM;

KNOWING THE SELF IS ENLIGHTENMENT.

And an overquoted, but nethertheless personal Bean Curd Boxing favorite:

IN THE PURSUIT OF LEARNING, EVERYDAY SOMETHING IS ACQUIRED.

IN THE PURSUIT OF THE TAO, EVERYDAY SOMETHING IS DROPPED.

Each Chapter contains so much simple wisdom, as valid for our digital lifestyles today as it was over 2.500 years ago.

Taoism experiences waves of popularity during different social and political eras. Recently it has experienced another resurgence due to its ecological roots, anti-consumerism and the resounding echoes of its simple philosophy. For the Tai Chi practitioner of the 21st Century it offers a set of guidelines for living and working that are simultaneously ancient and modern, abstract and practical.

9. TAI CHI IN THE 21ST CENTURY

Q.44. Can you learn Tai Chi from a DVD?

A. Once upon a time we would ask: Is it possible to learn Tai Chi from a book? Then the question moved onto the video, DVD, web page, YouTube, holographic instructors or by setting up a Facebook group and learning a posture a day via twitter.

It may well be the case that any one of these tools, or all of them, may help you gain an understanding of Tai Chi, but in themselves they are unlikely to provide you with the fine adjustments to your posture and state of mind that only a real life teacher and classroom environment can impart. It is a good thing to have real people to work with, for it means real connections in real time. And the more people we have real contact with - like pebbles on a beach - the more we are shaped in turn by their contact with us. Digital learning may be of partial use, but in a class the experience is not just visual and audible, it is spoken and tactile too in an unpredictable way, and learning arises out of a hundred different events in a given moment.

If it were your only choice to learn by YouTube, then it may help those people that will never have an instructor close by. But if you wish for depth to your study, choose the real thing, for Tai Chi is alive and adapts to the moment like an adventure an adventure, a dialogue and a life-changing experience.

One final point to remember:

I've said it before, but it's worth repeating here: Try out more than one class if you can. Go visit a few, and see which one you are more attracted to.

Q.45. Speaking of DVD's, wasn't David Carradine a Master of teaching Tai Chi by DVD?

A. David Carradine was first and foremost an actor. As an actor he could explain and demonstrate well - for that was his profession. But his kung-fu performance lacked credibility in the eyes of other martial artists, who saw a man acting the part of a master, but displaying few of the skills.

After the Kung Fu series ended, David Carradine did study for a while with a number of proficient teachers. He had clearly been influenced by the series and wanted to understand more of the martial arts that he had come to symbolise for so many years. To give the man credit, he did actually play the flute on screen. Not only did he play the instrument but he grew the bamboo and carved the flute himself. He even planted bamboo on different parts of the Warner Brothers film set so he would be able to make a new flute wherever he was working at the time.

His on-screen life contrasted strongly with the martial artists that followed in his footsteps. Following from the huge publicity that Carradine generated through the Kung Fu series, skilled artists from all over the globe began to produce an endless stream of movies in which they were capable of delivering a convincing roundhouse kick, but when it came to delivering convincing dialogue, something was often amiss. Carradine could do that at least.

Sadly, Carradine may only be remembered for the things he wasn't - the 19th century Chinese-American that he wasn't, the Shaolin priest that he wasn't and the

Tai Chi master that he wasn't. Still, he could carve a fine flute and his presence in the Tarrantino films more than made up for his earlier transgressions.

Q.46. If David Carradine was not a true Tai Chi Master, how then can I recognise an Authentic Sage today?

A. Finding a contemporary sage has never been an easy task. They rarely advertise themselves on Facebook, nor does the genuine article appear on DVD, on the page of an on-line web training school, or in the poster of a new film to be released.

True teachers of wisdom may not even teach Tai Chi, for that is the conundrum of the age in which we live. What may be advertised as Tai Chi, may in fact be something else. A course on permaculture, a seminar on Chi Gung or a strategy for developing productivity by emptying your mind may, in fact, be far more sage-like and useful in content than purchasing the entire series of Kwai Chang Caine on Amazon.

Ultimately you will need to learn to recognise what is genuine and what is not. When looking for the right class to join, try watching to see who it is that grows bamboo and who doesn't, who expresses claims of invulnerability and who displays humility. In this age of unrestrained self-promotion you may have to look far to stumble upon such a class

Q.47. Some classes play music whilst practising Tai Chi. What role has rhythm in the learning of this Noble Art?

A. I remember in my youth learning Wing Chun to the sounds of Rap, and during the wild sparring sessions the music seemed to do little other than camouflage my screams as blows rained down on my confused limbs. Perhaps I had simply not learnt to yelp in time to the rhythm.

But in a Tai Chi class that has less structured training drills and sparring sessions, what role has an external rhythm in the class? One answer is to think of rhythm as something to help you find your inner timing.

If we are good practitioners, we attune ourselves to the rhythms of not just our own breath, but also the breath of those around us, the rhythm of the wind and the dance of light.

Remember: Tai Chi is not just about YOU. It is a 'Dialogue with Life'.

Traditionalists argue that using music is encouraging an artificial pace, and that you must find your own rhythm! To accomplish this, you must have quiet, and tranquility in the class.

But I would say: Yes, yes, yes. And while you are at it, don't forget to iron your satin Chinese tunic before you leave home...

Lets not forget we all learnt by following an artificial pace: The pace and rhythm of the instructor or the better student in class, the DVD or the YouTube video. (Sad I know, but people do). And I've had some instructors that although could deliver a mean one-inch punch - were incapable of a simple shuffle.

So...if you wish to learn about attuning yourself to rhythm then let your body follow the pulse. Allow your breathing and movements to align themselves and in that process, learn to adjust, adapt and follow rhythms that are not always yours. The secret is simply to stay loose, stay light and learn to take your root with you.

Adaptability is the key and the better we are at adapting to different rhythms...dare I say it...even broken rhythms, then the better we adapt to the ever varying rhythms of life.

Break with static.

Challenge the convention

It's a bit like Twitter: Follow, and in the process of following, adapt and learn until you have your own flow.

Q.48. What about applying all these principles to my work? Can Tai Chi work alongside a GTD approach?

A. Getting Things Done (GTD) is a productivity concept that originated with the publication in 2001 of David Allen's book of the same name. Allen's basic approach - compiled from a simple combination of Zen philosophy and management organisation tools - focuses on clearing your mind completely of any outstanding tasks.

He says that you need to file everything that comes into your

daily life: Everything needs either doing, deferring, delegating or deleting. If it can be done within a minute or two, then it should be done there and then. If it needs more thought or attention then defer it. If it needs another's participation first then delegate, otherwise delete it.

What is interesting about Allen's approach is that it talks about small incremental steps to accomplish long tern goals, as well as a reliable review system. He is also keen on using water as an analogy:

How, he asks, does water respond to a pebble thrown in? It sends out ripples, pebble size ripples, and then returns to a calm and quiet state. When a boulder lands, it responds with boulder ripples and then returns to a calm and tranquil state. What water does not do is tense up before the rock hits the surface. In short it is the art of training oneself in the perfectly appropriate response to, and engagement with, whatever is present.

Does this sound familiar in a wu wei sort of way?

Q.49. Would Lao Tzu have used GTD?

A. Well Lao Tzu said:

"DO THE DIFFICULT THINGS WHILE THEY ARE EASY AND DO THE GREAT THINGS WHILE THEY ARE SMALL...A JOURNEY OF A THOUSAND MILES MUST BEGIN WITH A SINGLE STEP."

Sound familiar to Allen's small incremental steps?

Yet Lao Tzu's philosophy went beyond systems. He said: "nature does not hurry, yet everything is accomplished."

This sounds just fine, and makes for nice quotes, but provides us with few clues as to how it is actually accomplished (other than by not rushing).

Now there's a thought: not rushing. Perhaps the answer can be found in moving at the appropriate speed. Let's return to the theme of slowing down once more.

When we move at an appropriate speed things remain clear, yet if we pick up speed then things turn into a blur. Think driving down a country lane versus driving down a motorway.

Q.50. What if I have not understood any of this?

A. Then just throw it all away. Throwing stuff away is a good thing for it leaves room for something else.

> "The true harvest
> of my life is
> intangible -- a
> little star dust
> caught,
> a portion of the
> rainbow
> I have clutched"
>
> Henry David Thoreau

Reputedly, when Confucius asked Lao Tsu about the performing of rites and rituals, Lao Tzu replied: "The bones of the people you are talking about have long since turned to dust! Only their words linger on."

Going beyond lingering words is a lesson we too often ignore. If instead of obsessing over the right phrase, we look for a sense of balance, a deeper breath or a softness in our glare, then perhaps another language will have the room to emerge. It's about finding the courage to let go of certainty. Its about opening doors that have traditionally been closed, stepping through and seeing what may come about.

There is an exercise in Tai Chi called "Listening". It is about learning to learn with more than just your mind. If Tai Chi is about anything, it is about the application of this lesson.

Q.51. (Bonus Question for having reached the end!) Why would you let go of the things you are certain about?

A. Letting go by itself is a useful habit. When we let go, we allow for a change of direction. When we let go of what we are, we become what we might be, said Lao Tzu. Other ideas and sensations have room to pass by without judgment, without censorship. At times, that's just what we need, even though we don't know it, because our words have told us otherwise.

10. GOING BEYOND THE WORDS

So is Tai Chi a Martial Art, a Health art or a philosophical point of view? Is Tai Chi an ancient art or a contemporary practice? Is it now oriental or occidental? Hopefully, some of these 50 questions and answers have helped you come to your own conclusions about this Noble Art. But, one last word of caution, if you are still looking for absolutes, certainties and fixed ideas then Tai Chi may come as a surprise to you. On the surface it all looks so mechanical and precise, yet underneath it is an unstable pattern of forms and energy that is never completely still or fixed.

Its inherent flexibility, diverse origins and open philosophy has meant that Tai Chi has adapted to different times, cultures and locations over its long history. Some have argued that this has diluted its original message and skill base. Others, in reply, have said that such diversity has  ensured its continuation, growth and ability to stay relevant in the 21st century.

Each year, as the planet becomes increasingly digitalized, people are becoming hungrier for a sense of connection with something profound, something timeless and something that can inspire rather than simply entertain us for 10 minutes.

Tai Chi may well form an integral part of that offering. Now, go find a class.

FOLLOW YOUR BREATH

ABOUT PAUL READ

Although I was born in London, England I am now living and working as a teacher, translator and writer in the Granada area of Andalusia in southern Spain. As a life-long martial artist, I have worn many hats during my working life, but none so enthusiastically as that of teacher of Tai Chi, for it has taught me that although knowledge is relatively easy to come-by, wisdom remains as elusive as ever

CONNECT WITH THE AUTHOR

Web:

http://www.teapotmonk.com/

Facebook:

http://www.facebook.com/TheBeanCurdBoxer

Twitter:

http://twitter.com/BeanCurdBoxer

YouTube:

http://www.youtube.com/user/teapotmonk

LinkedIn:

http://es.linkedin.com/pub/paul-read/31/615/96

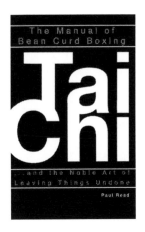

OTHER BOOKS BY PAUL READ

The Manual of Bean Curd Boxing:

Tai Chi and the Noble Art of leaving Things Undone

This is a Manual for 21st Century Living. Redefining the lessons of Taoism and the practical exercises of Tai Chi, this book describes how to use the most practical points from these ancient disciplines to enable us to reach out and grasp life with more energy, with more passion and with more wisdom. Instead of acquiring yet more tools, throw them away and learn the Art of Leaving Things Undone.

REVIEWS FOR MANUAL OF BEAN CURD BOXING:

Bob Klein, author of the classic Tai Chi text: Movements of Power and Movements of Magic.

"...A great contribution to the world of Tai Chi...It is rare that I actually enjoy a Tai Chi book, most are a regurgitation of others...but I greatly enjoyed The Manual of Bean Curd Boxing."

" It is a great introduction to Tai Chi...it is also a book for anyone to get an insight into a different point of view of life."

Buck Barnes Tai Chi Teacher, Atlanta, Georgia.

"...Paul Read doesn't promise enlightenment in Bean Curd Boxer yet I am enlightened from reading it.."

It is the most important and helpful tai chi for life book I have read in years.

" It brings me along, one careful cat step further, on my never-ending tai chi journey. Excuse me now, I'm off to gently fry a small fish."

Printed in Great Britain
by Amazon

43801279R00066